A
SYSTEM
OF
TARGET PRACTICE.

FOR THE USE OF TROOPS

WHEN ARMED WITH THE MUSKET, RIFLE-MUSKET, RIFLE, OR CARBINE.

PREPARED PRINCIPALLY FROM THE FRENCH.

PUBLISHED BY ORDER OF THE WAR DEPARTMENT.

WASHINGTON:
GOVERNMENT PRINTING OFFICE.
1862.

WAR DEPARTMENT,

WASHINGTON, *May* 30, 1862.

THIS system of Target Practice, prepared under direction of the War Department, having been approved, is adopted for the instruction of troops, when armed with the Musket, Rifle Musket, Rifle, or Carbine.

EDWIN M. STANTON,
Secretary of War.

CONTENTS.

TARGET PRACTICE.

FIRST LESSON.

Exercise Preparatory to Firing.

SECOND LESSON.

Firing with Ball Cartridges at different Distances, and Formation of Classes.

THIRD LESSON.

Firing as Skirmishers.

FOURTH LESSON.

Firing by File, by Company or Rank, and by Platoon.

LIST OF FORMS.

LIST OF PLATES.

Target Practice.

THE inaccuracy of the soldiers of our army in firing has been a matter of surprise and regret to many officers. This has been especially remarked upon since the introduction of the expanding ball into our service.

When we reflect that many of the rank and file composing our army have never fired a gun previous to their enlistment, indeed, that some have never had a gun in their hands, it would be truly surprising were such men good shots.

The slow progress in attaining any thing like precision in firing is believed attributable, in a great measure, to ignorance of those principles which must govern all good marksmen when firing, the chief of which is a knowledge of aiming the piece correctly.

Persons accustomed to the use of fire-arms from their youth find no difficulty in aiming a gun correctly at an object. Not so, however, with the man who has never handled a gun. As simple as this appears, some men never can acquire it.

It will be found very generally to be a fact, that a soldier who habitually fires inaccurately has no idea of the principles which should govern him in aiming his piece.

An officer standing in the rear, or in front, of a man when aiming cannot detect inaccuracies of aim; but, if the soldier is made to place his gun on a suitable rest, and aim it at an object, the officer will immediately detect all errors, which having been pointed out, the soldier receives a useful lesson in aiming his piece, which it will be easy for him to carry out when aiming from a prescribed position.

In order that fire-arms in the hands of soldiers may produce their full effect, it is necessary,

1st. That the soldier should have sufficient knowledge of the parts of his piece to enable him to take it apart and put it together again for the purpose of keeping it in order.

2d. That the soldier should know how to load his gun properly.*　The School of the Soldier contains all that is necessary on this subject.

3d. That the rules for firing his piece should be known; that is to say, that he knows the manner of regulating his aim according to the distance of the object to be hit.

4th. That he should be practised in estimating distances within the range of his piece.

5th. That he should be able to take a position which enables him,

To aim with ease;

To keep the body steady, without constraint;

Not to incline the sights to the right or left;

To support the recoil.

6th. When pressing on the trigger to discharge the piece, not to derange his aim.

The above comprises all that is necessary for the soldier to know, and put in practice, in order that he may obtain the maximum effect of his arm.

By examining the details of instruction as given above, it will be seen that, in order that a soldier may be made familiar with them, it is not necessary to fire in reality.

The soldier should acquire the above by degrees. If the soldier's attention be at first confined to aiming his piece,

---

* An officer, *en route* to New Mexico with some two hundred recruits, reported that, having had occasion to examine the pieces of the men, he found at least one hundred pieces loaded with the ball-end of the cartridge inserted first.

he will more readily acquire this than if he were required to aim, and to take a prescribed position at the same time. Having acquired a knowledge of the principles of aiming his piece, and then a prescribed position, he will readily acquire the habit of aiming correctly from this position.

He should now learn the proper manner of pulling the trigger, and, when putting this in practice, to keep his piece steady.

The soldier will next be taught to support the recoil, and become accustomed to the report of his piece, by first using caps, and then blank cartridges.

Such appears to be the natural order of instruction to overcome the difficulties attending the proper use of his arm when firing. It is asserted, by the English and French, that soldiers, by the above course of instruction, have been made good shots without having fired a single ball.

In the spring of 1856, a company in our service, drilled in a similar manner, improved three hundred per cent. in accuracy of fire in six weeks' time.

The necessity of soldiers being able to estimate distances with some degree of accuracy is very evident. Without such knowledge, no accuracy of fire could be obtained when deployed as skirmishers; as the soldier is then compelled to rely upon his own judgment.

If to the above we join sufficient theoretical instruction strictly necessary to enable the soldier to aim his piece correctly, according to the distance of the object to be hit, we will certainly obtain, when firing, results far superior to those which would be obtained by passing immediately from the School of the Soldier to firing at a target. The instruction would not be complete if a soldier were only made to fire from the position which he would naturally take when standing, and not in ranks; or, in other words, when firing as a skirmisher, standing. Instruction in firing by file, by company, or rank, and by platoon, is necessary to complete the course.

The following practice will be repeated annually. The practice should commence as soon after January as possible.

At many of our Western posts game is abundant. Commanding officers are recommended to encourage the men to hunt; and for this purpose they are authorized to issue a small quantity of ammunition.

First Lesson.

EXERCISE PREPARATORY TO FIRING.

In the exercises which constitute this lesson, the company will be divided into as many squads as there are instructors available. When the exercise is conducted on the drill-ground, the squads will be formed in one rank, with an interval of one pace between the files, and equipped as for drill. The bayonet, as a general rule, will be in the scabbard, unless otherwise directed.

ARTICLE I.

AIMING.

Instruction in aiming will be given at first in the quarters, if practicable. A bag, partially filled with sand or earth, is placed on a bench, the bench on a table: by striking the bag with the back of the hand, an indentation will be formed in which the piece can be rested. The piece is now placed on the bag, and aimed by the instructor on some object, such as a wafer on the wall, being careful that the sights incline neither to the right or left. He now points out to his squad the two points which determine the line of sight; that is, the top of the front or muzzle-sight, and the middle of the

Plate I,

notch of the hausse or breech-sight. The instructor explains that aiming consists in bringing these two points, and the object aimed at, in the same right line.

Each man, in turn, placing himself behind the butt of the piece, without touching it, closing the left eye, looks through the middle of the notch of the breech-sight, over the top of the front sight, and on the centre of the wafer upon which the line of sight was previously directed, and satisfies himself that these three points are in the same right line, (see Plate 1.) The instructor will now derange the gun, and then call up each soldier in turn, who will aim the piece at the point indicated: he will criticize the aiming, pointing out to each of them their error or errors, if any are found, by making them see that the object aimed at is not in the line of sight, but that this line passes to the right, left, above, or below, as the case may be. After having rectified the aiming of each soldier, the instructor will be careful to derange the piece. This exercise will be repeated; but, instead of the instructor rectifying errors himself, he will first call up the men of his squad in turn, and ask each if the line of sight passes to right, left, above, or below the point indicated, or whether the piece inclines to the right or left. When the men have expressed their opinions, the instructor will give his own, correcting thus all the errors which have been committed. The instructor will repeat this exercise as often as may be necessary. After each drill, the instructor will enter, in a note-book, good, medium, or bad aiming, opposite each man's name.

Two drills, of two hours each, devoted to the first part of the instruction in aiming, will be sufficient to teach the generality of men the principles of aiming a gun with the raised sight down.

In a third drill, the instructor will explain to his squad the use of the different parts of his piece, the rules for firing, the object and use of the raised sight, by tracing the following figure on a board, table, or floor. Explain that the line of

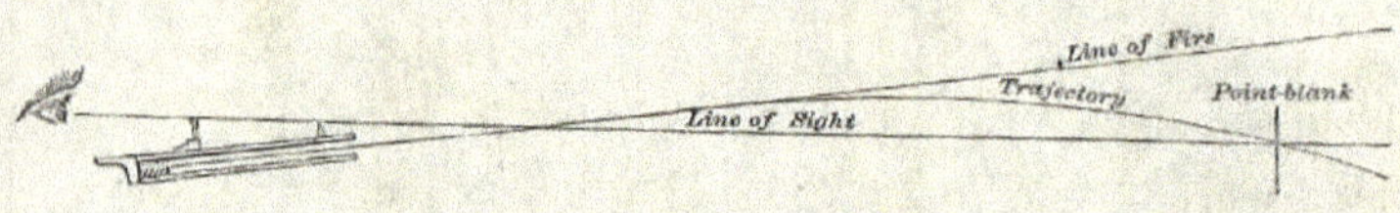

fire is the axis of the gun indefinitely produced, that the ball describes a curved line during its flight, that the line of sight is a right line passing through the middle of the notch of the rear sight and the top of front sight, that the point-blank is the second intersection of the trajectory, or curve, with the line of sight. Assuming the point-blank of a gun, with the hausse down, to be 200 yards, he will explain to his squad, that to hit a man in the head at 200 yards, aim at his head; at 150, at his throat; at 100, at his chest, and so on. Thus, with the assistance of a curved line, and a few simple remarks adapted to the comprehension of any man of ordinary intelligence, the squad will receive a lesson which many will find useful in practice, and but few will forget. The instructor will, from time to time during the drill, question the men, and satisfy himself that he is clearly understood. The instructor will also add, that, by the use of the hausse or raised sight, the number of points-blank are increased, and explain the reason.

The fourth, fifth, and sixth drills that follow will take place on the drill-ground, and squads will be exercised in aiming at any distance between 100 and 1000 yards, or up to that point for which the arm is sighted. Each squad is provided with a target, a bag partially filled with sand, and a tripod, formed of poles about six feet long, tied or fastened near the top. The tripod is placed in an upright position, the sand-bag on the tripod, and the piece on the sand-bag. Each man aims his own gun, (see Plate 2.) When he pronounces his piece correctly aimed, the instructor calls up the remainder of the squad in turn, who examine the piece and

Plate II.

inform the instructor, in a low tone, how, in their opinion, the gun is sighted. The instructor notes down their answers in his note-book. He then examines the piece himself, pronounces how the gun is aimed, calls up those who answered incorrectly, and, having satisfied them of their errors, requires the man who aimed the piece to correct his mistake. At the end of the drill the instructor will note good, medium, or bad aiming opposite each man's name. Should the captain of the company require it, the note-books used by the instructors during drill will be handed to him after drill. Should it be desirable to economize targets, one ,target will answer for the different squads of the same company during this part of the drill: in that case the tripods will be placed as near together as practicable. Soldiers who have previously been thoroughly instructed in this part of the exercise, and show a knowledge of the first four drills, may be excused from the last two.

ARTICLE II.

POSITION OF A SKIRMISHER AIMING STANDING.

When the men can aim correctly from a rest, they will be instructed in the above position.

Squads under arms will be formed in a single rank, with an interval of one pace between the files.

The instructor, facing the squad, will give the details of the position, executing the same himself as he describes them.

AIMING WITH SIGHT DOWN, (WHEN RIFLED MUSKET IS USED.)

ONE TIME AND THREE MOTIONS.

First Motion.—As first motion of "charge bayonet," Scott's Tactics, vol. i. paragraph 187, except that the right foot is carried fifteen inches to rear of left heel.

Second Motion.—Bring down the piece with the right hand to the right side, the barrel uppermost; seizing it with the left hand in rear of the hausse or breech-sight, the stock resting in the palm of this hand, the thumb extended along the stock, the left elbow close to the body, the muzzle as high as the eye. Cock the piece with the thumb of the right hand, the fingers supported against the guard and the small of the stock; seize the piece at the small of the stock with the right hand.

Third Motion.—Turn in slightly the left toe, raise the piece with both hands; place the butt firmly against the shoulder, the body erect, the left elbow close to the body; shut the right eye, raise the right shoulder in order to bring the sight to the height of the right eye, the elbow raised nearly to the height of the shoulder; aim, keeping the line of sight horizontal and in the vertical plane of fire, inclining as little as possible the head to the right, the thumb of the right hand over the small of the stock, the last joint of the first finger of the right hand in front of but not touching the trigger, the remaining fingers under, and grasping the small of the stock.

AIMING WITH SIGHT DOWN, (WHEN RIFLE IS USED.)

ONE TIME AND THREE MOTIONS.

First Motion.—Raise the piece with the right hand; make a half-face to the right on the left heel; place the hollow of the right foot opposite to, and fifteen inches from, left heel; the feet square: seize the piece at the same time with the left hand in rear of the hausse or breech-sight, the thumb extending along the stock.

Second Motion.—Bring down the piece with both hands; the barrel uppermost, the left elbow close to the body, the muzzle as high as the eye. Cock the piece with the thumb of the right hand, the fingers supported against the guard and the small of the stock. Seize the piece at the small of the stock with the right hand.

Third Motion.—Same as that given for rifled musket.

The instructor directs each man to take the position, commencing on the right of the squad : during the instruction he will assist the soldier in supporting his arm by placing his right hand under or near the middle band. After which, the man is made to take the position without any assistance. The commands given in order to make a soldier take or abandon the positions as given above, will be,—

" As a skirmisher, aim."

" Cease—aiming."

At the first part of the last command, withdraw the finger from in front of the trigger ; at the command "Aiming," retake the position of the second motion of "Aiming with sight down ;" half-cock the piece, and come to a shoulder. As the instructor proceeds with the squad, he will direct those who have been instructed to exercise themselves in taking the position, keeping it for an instant, and then abandoning it, repeating this as often as they can while the rest are being instructed. Men will be cautioned not to cock the piece when repeating the instruction. The squad will now be exercised in aiming together, keeping them in the position long enough to confirm, but not long enough to fatigue them. This drill may be conducted in the quarters. In this case the instructor will drill but one man at a time ; the remainder will exercise themselves in taking and abandoning the position as he proceeds. Two drills will be given to the above exercise. One will suffice for soldiers who have been previously instructed.

During the drill, the soldier will not be required to aim at any fixed point, the object being, that he may acquire with ease the position of a soldier, "aiming as a skirmisher, standing," and the habit of readily catching with his eye the two points which determine the line of sight.

When the men are confirmed in the position described above, they will be exercised at aiming at a mark. First, with the sight down : one drill will be given to this exercise.

Previous to the man's aiming, the instructor will order him to direct the line of sight below the point to be aimed at; to raise the piece slowly until the line of sight is on the point designated, preserving his aim for an instant, keeping the body and gun immovable. During the first part of this drill the men will be instructed individually.

The men will now be exercised in aiming, using the hausse for ranges for which it is graduated, and the intermediate ones

AIMING WITH SIGHT RAISED, (WHEN RIFLE MUSKET AND RIFLE ARE USED.)

ONE TIME AND FOUR MOTIONS.

First and Second.—Same as "Aiming with sight down."

Third Motion.—Raise the piece slightly with both hands, at the same time depressing the muzzle until the piece is horizontal, the left arm and stock against the body: with the thumb and first finger of the right hand, regulate the hausse for the distance indicated, and seize the piece with the right hand at the small of the stock.

Fourth Motion.—Same as third motion, "Aiming with sight down."

Two drills will be given to this exercise: during the first drill, the men will be instructed individually, commencing with the lower sights, and then causing the hausse to be raised gradually.

The position of a soldier aiming as a skirmisher cannot always be taken exactly in the same manner, as it will be found necessary to lower the shoulder and arms in proportion as the hausse is elevated: without moving the body, or inclining the head, the soldier, by lowering the shoulder and arms, can take any line of sight from 250 to 1000 yards. This will be found a good exercise for the men. In order to aim at objects 800, 900, and 1000 yards distant, it is necessary to press the heel of the butt of the piece against the shoulder. If men have short necks, the position is constrained, and cannot be taken properly. Instructors perceiving this difficulty will exercise their judgment in requiring men to take the position above designated when firing at these long ranges.

During the second drill, squads formed on the drill-ground will be exercised in aiming together, using the different lines of sight for which the hausse is regulated. In this drill the bayonet will be fixed when aiming at distances less than 400 yards.

ARTICLE III.

POSITION OF A SOLDIER KNEELING AND AIMING AS A SKIRMISHER.

The instruction will be given without times or motions. The instructor will command,

"Take the position of a skirmisher kneeling and aiming," or, "Cease aiming."

The instructor will detail the position of a skirmisher kneeling and aiming, as follows. The squad is supposed to be at shouldered arms, the files one pace apart. Take the position of present-arms; then carry the right foot to the rear and to the right of the left heel, and in a position convenient for placing the right knee upon the ground in bending the left leg; place the right knee upon the ground, lower the piece, the left forearm supported upon the thigh on the same side, the right hand on the small of the stock, the butt resting on the right thigh, the left hand supporting the piece near the lower band. Move the right leg to the left, around the knee supported on the ground, until this leg is nearly perpendicular to the direction of the left foot, and thus seat himself on the right heel. Raise the piece with the right hand and support it with the left, holding it near the lower band, the left elbow resting on the left thigh near the knee. With the thumb and forefinger of the right hand regulate the hausse, if necessary; cock the piece, seize it with the right hand at the small of the stock, the right shoulder raised or lowered according to the position of the target, the right elbow nearly to the height of the shoulder; aim at the point indicated, keeping the top of the muzzle-sight and the bottom of the notch of the hausse in the vertical plane of fire, the thumb of the right hand over the small of the stock, the last joint of the first finger of the right hand in front of but not touching the trigger, the other fingers of this hand grasping the small of the stock. The instructor, having taken, and detailed at the same time, the position of a skirmisher kneeling and aiming, will instruct the men in aiming from this position, in conformity with what has been prescribed in Article II. Two drills will be given to this exercise. One will suffice for soldiers previously instructed in the drill.

ARTICLE IV.

KEEPING THE PIECE STEADY WHEN THE TRIGGER IS PULLED.

It is easy to preserve the aim until the trigger is pressed upon in order to discharge the piece; but, when this is done, the aim is maintained with difficulty. When pressing on the trigger, the line of sight is apt to be deranged: although properly directed before touching the trigger, it may not be so at the moment the discharge takes place. The report of the discharge of his piece should find the soldier still preserving his aim. The soldier will attain this if he holds his breath from the moment he commences to touch the trigger until the gun is discharged; if he does not pull the trigger with a jerk, or suddenly, but increases the pressure on the trigger by degrees; if he places his finger in such a manner upon the trigger as to exercise its full force, pressing not on the extremity of the finger, but on the last joint, or as near this joint as the conformation of the man will permit. The instructor, holding a gun in a convenient position similar to that of charge-bayonet, will point out to each soldier in succession the manner of pulling the trigger, which will be done with the first finger of the right hand as described above, the remaining fingers of this hand under and grasping the small of the stock, the thumb over the stock.

The men repeat after the instructor, in succession, what he has just executed. After this has been repeated as often as necessary, the instructor explains to his squad how they should manage in order to fire without deranging the position of the piece after bringing the line of sight to bear on an object. He will explain and execute this as follows, aiming as in Article II.

Press upon the trigger by degrees with the last joint of the first finger of the right hand, closing the muscles of this finger without moving the arm, holding the breath, the sound of the discharge finding the soldier preserving the line of sight upon the point aimed at. Remain aiming an instant after the gun is discharged, to be assured that the object is still in the line of sight. In actual firing, it will be impossible to preserve the aim the instant the gun is discharged; but, should the gun hang fire, the soldier accustomed to remain an instant aiming will be more apt to make a good shot.

The instructor should make the soldier understand that a good marksman is known by the steadiness with which he preserves his gun when it misses fire.

The men will be made to take one, or the other, of the positions of a soldier aiming, as laid down in Article II. They will be permitted to snap the gun without any commands being given to that effect. The instructor will indicate the distance, either assumed or real, of the target, and will see that the men use the sights corresponding to those distances. The instructor will command, for instance, "Take the position of a 'skirmisher aiming standing' at 600 yards' aim."

The exercise given in this article is considered of great importance. It will be repeated for four drills. Two will suffice for those men who have been previously instructed.

ARTICLE V.

SIMULATED FIRING WITH CAPS.

This article is the same as the preceding, except that a cap will be used, and it will not be necessary to explain to the soldier the manner of pulling the trigger. Squads assembled in the quarters will be made to aim at a lighted candle, which will be placed three feet or more from the muzzle of the gun. The line of sight will be brought to bear below the flame; then, gradually raising the piece until the line of sight is directly on the flame, the cap will be exploded : if the cone and barrel of the piece are perfectly clear, and the piece correctly sighted, the body kept steady when aiming and at the moment the cap explodes, the candle will be extinguished. Simulated firing with caps will be executed in two drills. Ten caps per man will be exploded at each drill; eight caps standing and two kneeling.

ARTICLE VI.

SIMULATED FIRING WITH BLANK CARTRIDGES.

Firing with blank cartridges will be conducted in conformity with the principles laid down in the foregoing articles. The squad will be formed on the drill-ground as prescribed in Article II. The men will fire in succession at a target, placed or supposed to be placed at different distances. The rules laid down in the foregoing articles relating to a soldier aiming will be strictly followed. This lesson will be executed in two drills; ten cartridges will be fired per man at each drill; eight standing and two kneeling.

The object of these drills is to accustom the men to preserve their aim when firing.

Plate III.

ARTICLE VII.

ESTIMATING DISTANCES.

(See Plate 3.)

The company assembled fully equipped as for drill will be divided into at least three squads, or as many as there are company officers present. Each officer is provided with a small cord, 25 yards long. The instructor will measure on the ground a right line, which will be marked off into distances,

0, 50, 100, 150, 200, yards; 0, 50, 100, 150, 200,

marking these distances, as measured, with a stake, stone, or line, on the ground. He will now direct each man of his squad to pace off the measured distance of 100 yards, cautioning them to be careful and preserve their natural gait, without attempting to increase or diminish the length of their step. He will direct the men to count the number of steps they take in passing over the distance of 100 yards. This having been repeated at least three times by each soldier, who reports each time the number of steps taken by him in passing over 100 yards, the ratio which a yard bears to the step of each soldier becomes known. The instructor will inform each soldier the number of steps it will be necessary for him to take to pass over 10 yards. The soldier now knowing the number of steps he must take to pass over 10 and 100 yards, it will be easy for him to measure any distance with sufficient accuracy for all practical purposes when firing.

To estimate a distance greater than 100 yards—in steps—the soldier, having started from the point of departure, will count the number of steps he should take to pass over 100 yards; extending as a tally, at the moment of arrival, the thumb of his right hand, the other fingers closed: he will recommence then his count, extending the first finger of the right hand when he has counted the number of steps necessary to make a second 100 yards, and so on, until he arrives at a point less than 100 yards from the point up to which he is to measure. When the soldier finds himself less than 100 yards from the object, he will count by tens, saying, "Ten yards," when he has counted the number of steps necessary for him to pass over the distance of 10 yards, 20, 30 yards, and so on, until he arrives very near the object, when he will increase the length of his step, counting each step a yard; and, by adding these to the tens, he will then only have to count as hundreds the number of fingers he has raised, to know the whole distance, expressed in yards.

The instructor will form his squad at one of the extremities of the 200 yard line, which has been measured in such a way that the right line measured shall be perpendicular to the front of the squad. He will order four men to place themselves, the first at the point marked 50 yards, the second at the point marked 100 yards, the third at the point marked 150 yards, and the fourth at the point marked 200 yards. The men selected should be as near the same height as practicable. The instructor will now direct the attention of the squad to the different parts of the dress, arms, equipment, and figure of the men on the line, such as can be easily distinguished and recognised at 50 yards, and such as cannot be readily recognised at this distance. He questions each man of his squad on these points, not expecting all to answer alike, since the eyesight of men will generally differ.

The instructor will now call the attention of the men to the soldier placed at the point 100 yards distant, and cause them to make similar observations upon this man as those already prescribed for the soldier at 50 yards. The instructor again questions the men, and will be careful to point out to them the difference that exists between those two distances, as illustrated by the difference in the appearance of the same objects at these distances. The instructor will make, in succession, upon the two men placed at 150 and 200 yards, similar observations as prescribed for the men at 50 and 100 yards;

being very careful to call the attention of each man to the difference which exists between the four distances, illustrated by the distinctness with which certain objects are seen. The instructor will direct the squad to notice that men appear smaller the farther they are off, although in reality they are nearly the same height. The men stationed at the different points will be frequently replaced by others. When the men of the squad have made a sufficient number of observations upon the four distances above indicated, and when these observations are well impressed on their memories, the instructor will cause the squad to estimate intermediate distances between 50 and 200 yards.

In order to do this, the instructor will march his squad to a different part of the ground from that on which he measured the distances in the first instance, and form it in one rank. He now sends out one man, directing him to halt at a given signal. The instant this man steps off, the squad is faced about, in order that the men may not count the steps taken. When the man proceeds a sufficient distance, he will be halted, facing towards the squad. The squad will now be faced to the front. The men will estimate the distance which separates them from the soldier. The instructor cautions the squad to recollect the observations made by them upon the men placed at the measured distances. The instructor, placing himself a short distance from the squad, calls each man to him in turn, directing them to give in their estimates in a low voice. This is necessary, in order that no man may be influenced in his judgment by the opinion of another. The instructor writes in his note-book, opposite each man's name, the distance as estimated by him. The instructor will now cause the distance to be measured, and, at the same time, stepped off by the men. The instructor, having received from each man the distance as measured by him, will insert the same, by the side of the distance as estimated. The instructor now points out to the men the errors, if any were committed, in estimating the distance. In order to do this more distinctly, he may send a man to the point from which the squad started, pointing out all errors by observations on this man. The instructor will repeat this exercise as often as in his judgment is necessary, taking care each time to choose a different distance, but always between the limits above indicated.

Estimating distances should take place under different conditions of the atmosphere, cloudy, foggy, &c.; and, if the locality permits, squads should be drilled on ground the outline of which is diversified by hills, ravines, &c.

When the instructor judges that the men of his squad—who should, if possible, be the same during these exercises—have acquired a sufficient accuracy in estimating distances comprised between 50 and 200 yards, he will proceed to estimate distances comprised between 200 and 400 yards. To accomplish this, he will cause to be measured a distance of 400 yards, and mark, upon the right line so measured, distances of 0, 200, 250, 300, 350, and 400 yards; 0, 200, 250, 300, 350, 400.

The squads will be formed as explained. The instructor now orders five men to place themselves, the 1st at 200, the 2d 250, the 3d 300, the 4th 350 and the 5th at 400 yards, facing the squad and resting on their arms. He will make upon these different distances observations similar to those already made upon the lesser distances and for that of 200 yards. This last distance should be the object of particular attention and study. The instructor will cause distances comprised between 200 and 400 yards to be estimated as explained for the lesser distances.

When the men have acquired sufficient accuracy in estimating distances comprised between 200 and 400 yards, they will be made to estimate distances comprised between 50 and 400 yards.

This having been accomplished, distances will be no longer estimated on single individuals, but on groups of men.

Each company, under the command of its captain, will be divided into two platoons; commanded by the first, and second lieutenants, when not superintending the firing of a class. The captain will keep himself with one of the two platoons, having an eye to the exercise. The chief of each platoon, having halted his platoon in a favorable position indicated by the captain, will bring his platoon to an order, and rest. A group, composed of a corporal, a drummer or bugler, and two men, will proceed immediately in front of the platoon, following a line indicated by the chief of platoon, who will point out to the corporal two points on this line upon which to direct himself. The corporal, having passed over a distance of 200 yards, but not exceeding 700, will be at liberty to halt his group. He will then place the men one pace apart, in one rank, and, facing the platoon, bring them to an order, and rest, and take his place on the right of the rank, the centre of which should be established on the line. The chief of the platoon will now estimate the distance himself, and note the same in his note-book. He will now call out the non-commissioned officers, receive their estimates, (which should be given in a low tone,) note down the same; and so on with the men. As soon as the officer in charge of the platoon commences to take down the estimates of the men, a sergeant, assisted by two men carrying a cord twenty-five yards long, will measure the distance which separates the platoon from the group, and note down the same.—Should the number of units which remain after having noted the hundreds and tens be less or equal to five, they will be rejected; if greater than five, they will be counted as ten. The officer having taken down the estimates, and the distance separating the platoon from the group having been measured, the officer will display a signal, and the sergeant who measured the distance will indicate the number of yards, by causing the drummer to sound a roll for each hundred, and a single tap for tens. The bugler will indicate the same by long and short notes.

The group, at the discretion of the officer commanding the platoon, may be made to increase or lessen the distance which separates it from the platoon, the corporal keeping the group within the limits prescribed, and on the line as indicated to him. When he halts the group, he will be careful to establish it on the line facing the platoon.

The sergeant charged with measuring the distance will retire a few paces from the line after having marked the point up to which he last measured.

He will observe the platoon, and as soon as its chief commences recording the estimates he will measure the distance which separates the group from its first station, taking note of this distance, and adding it to the first or subtracting it, as the case may be.

In estimating distances comprised between 700 and 1000 yards, the number composing a group will be increased to eight men, a corporal, and drummer or bugler. The groups will be formed sometimes in one and sometimes in two ranks.

In all other respects the rules laid down for estimating distances between 200 and 700 yards will be followed.

Instruction in estimating distances will be given when it does not interfere with other parts of the soldiers' drill. It will, however, always precede ball-practice, and be carried on during this practice. When one squad is occupied in firing at the target, the remaining squads will be exercised in estimating distances.

Officers, particularly, should be prompt in estimating distances correctly, as they are called upon to conduct and regulate the fire in presence of an enemy.

Second Lesson.

FIRING WITH BALL CARTRIDGES AT DIFFERENT DISTANCES, FORMATION OF CLASSES, ETC.

THE distances at which the targets are placed will be 150, 225, 250, 300, 325, 350, 400, 450, 500, 550, 600, 700, 800, 900, and 1000 yards.

These distances will be carefully measured and staked off on the "firing-ground."

The surfaces fired at will be,

at 150 and 225	yards one target 6 ft. high and 22 in. broad.
225 and 300	" one " " 44 "
325, 350, and 400	" one " " 66 "
450 and 500	" one " " 88 "
550 and 600	" one " " 110 "
700	" one " " 132 "
800	" one " " 176 "
900	" one " " 220 "
1000	" one " " 264 "

Four rounds will be fired at each of the above distances. The company will be divided into three equal classes, non-commissioned officers equally distributed. (See Form I.)

After the company has fired at the several distances 150, 225, 250, 300, 325, 350, and 400 yards, the classes will be rearranged according to merit of firing,—the first class composed of those men who have hit the target the greatest number of times, the second class of those who come next in order, and so on with the third, keeping the classes as nearly equal as practicable. Non-commissioned officers will not be assigned to classes according to merit, but according to rank, a sergeant in each class, the presence of non-commissioned officers being necessary with classes when estimating distances, &c. When the firing has been executed at the fifteen distances, the classes will be again reformed, as prescribed above; previous to which no change will be made.

Men who from unavoidable causes have missed drills will be placed in that class to which the number of their shots that hit the target entitles them,—which will be determined by a simple calculation.

A list of the company, arranged by classes, will be kept exposed in the quarters until new lists are formed. The object in forming classes is that the officers may know the good marksmen in their companies, and to stimulate the pride of the men.

When the company arrives on the ground, the classes will be paraded. The first class, formed in one rank, will take position ten steps in rear of the point from which the firing takes place, the centre of the rank on and perpendicular to the plane of fire.

The remaining classes will be divided into as many squads per class as there are intelligent non-commissioned officers available, and these squads, superintended by an officer, will be exercised, on suitable ground near the firing-ground, in estimating distances, or in what is laid down in Article IV. When estimating distances greater than 400 yards, the two classes may be united, in which case the detachment will be commanded by an officer. The officer superintending the firing will order his class to load at will, and then bring them to a "support arms," or "order arms," and rest.

Before a man fires, a roll on the drum, or note on the bugle, will be sounded. At this signal the markers will take their places. At the command

"Commence firing," the man on the right will take the position in front of the squad that has been pointed out to him, and fire, retiring, as soon as he has fired, three paces in rear of his first position; and so on with the rest. When a class has fired, it will reload at the commands "Load at will," "Load," and thus continue until the four shots have been expended.   Three shots will be fired standing, the fourth kneeling.   The firing of the other classes will be conducted in the same manner.   Officers should retire a short distance from the soldier who is about to fire, and be careful not to speak to him when in the act of firing.   Officers will pay particular attention that all the principles are followed which have been laid down in the foregoing articles.

Balls which strike within the black lines will have no greater value on the "record-book" than those which strike any other part of the target.

An intelligent non-commissioned officer, assisted by a man, will place themselves in a hole dug at the foot and in front of the target, protected by a breast work of earth thrown upon that side from which the firing takes place.   This non-commissioned officer will mark the shots which strike the target. He will be provided with a small flag, and a rod about six feet long, on one end of which will be nailed a circular disk of wood, or other material, six or eight inches in diameter, painted on one side white, on the other black.   When a ball strikes outside the black, he will cover the shot-hole with the disk, presenting the black side to the detachment; when inside the black, the white side will be presented to view.   Firing will only be permitted when the flag is down.   The marker should be provided with a pot of paste, a brush, and patches of paper, when the target covered with muslin is used.   After five shots, the marker will paste patches over the ball-holes, or otherwise deface them.   When cast-iron targets are used, the marker should be provided with black and white paint.

Should it not be possible to obtain the greatest range laid down, the entire number of shots will nevertheless be fired. The shots, in that case, will be divided equally between the 150 yard range and the greatest available range.

The officer superintending the drill will note opposite each man's name his *hits*, which, after the drill ends, will be copied in the record-book kept for that purpose.   (See Form I.)

When the first class has nearly completed firing its four rounds, the drummer will be directed to sound a roll, or the bugler the signal "Commence firing."

The second class will then be marched to the position occupied by the first, and execute what has been laid down above

During the remainder of the drill, the first class will be exercised in estimating distances. It will be found to economize time, and . the record of shots can be better kept, by keeping the same non-commissioned officer superintending the marking of shots during the entire drill.

Third Lesson.

FIRING AS SKIRMISHERS.

THE company will now be exercised in firing as skirmishers. Three drills will be given to this exercise. Ten cartridges will be fired per man at each drill. When firing as skirmishers, the men will be permitted to take that position which suits them best. The line of skirmishers will fire first advancing, then retreating, conforming to the principles laid down in the "instruction for skirmishers." The targets will be six feet high and twenty-two inches wide, placed upon a line parallel to the line of skirmishers and six yards apart.

As many targets will be used as the nature of the ground and a due regard to economy will permit. A line will be staked off parallel to the line of targets and 350 yards distant. The line of skirmishers, formed a suitable distance from this line, will advance upon it, and when on the line the command will be given, " Commence firing:" the line of skirmishers will advance and fire five rounds; the remaining five will be fired retreating.

The firing during the second drill will be executed as laid down for the first. The surface fired at will be double; the

targets placed six yards apart.   The firing will commence
when the skirmishers arrive on a line 600 yards from the
targets.   The number of targets will not be limited.   Five
cartridges will be fired advancing, and five retreating.

Firing during the third drill will commence when the skirmishers reach a line 800 yards from the line of targets.   Four
targets will be used, placed 12 yards apart.   The dimension
of each target will be 6 feet by 88 inches.   After each drill,
the distance at which the line of skirmishers commenced fire,
the number of men present at the drill, and the number of
balls that strike the targets, will be entered in the "record-
book." (See Form II.) When the ranges as laid down cannot
be obtained, they will be approximated to as nearly as possible,
and the prescribed number of shots fired.

Fourth Lesson.

FIRING BY COMPANY OR RANK, AND BY PLATOON.

THE exercises in firing will terminate with firing by file, by
company or rank, according to the tactics used, and by platoon.
At each drill, six cartridges per man will be fired by file, two
by rank or company, and two by platoon.   The distances at
which the several firings take place will be 300, 400, and 500
yards.   The target used will be 6 feet high and 176 inches
broad.   The vertical and horizontal stripes on this target will
be 12 inches in width.

The firings by file, by company or rank, and by platoon,
will be executed in three drills : at the first, the firing will
commence at 300 yards; the second, at 400; and the third,
at 500 yards.   At each drill, the firing will commence by file,
then by company or rank, and will end by firing by platoon.
When firing at 300 yards, whether by file, by company or

rank, or platoon, bayonets will be fixed. After each drill, the captain will enter in the "record-book" the number of men present at the drill, the number of balls fired, and the number that struck the target. (See Form III.) As the position of soldiers firing by file, company or rank, and by platoon, is different from that taken when firing as a skirmisher, it will be necessary, before executing the above firings, to habituate the men to the positions which they should take by simulated firings, such as have been described in Articles V. and VI. of First Lesson.

The simulated firing will first be by allowing the hammer to fall upon the cone. The men will be made to take the positions as laid down in the "School of a Soldier" as applicable to those different firings. They will be accustomed to regulate the hausse in ranks, putting in practice as much as possible, when firing in ranks, what has been prescribed for individual firing.

During the first part of the first drill, ten caps per man will be exploded,—six in file firing, two by company or rank, and two by platoon. During the second part of the same drill, ten blank cartridges will be fired,—six by file, two by company or rank, and two by platoon. The front rank will be made frequently to change positions with the rear rank. Firing with ball cartridges will then take place, preceding each real fire by simulated firings, when the hammer will be allowed to fall upon the cone. The proper execution of platoon and company firing depends in a great degree upon the commands of the officer. If he does not allow a sufficient interval between the commands "Aim" and "Fire," the men will not have time to aim. To obey in time the command, the trigger will be pulled suddenly. The result will be, that much of the efficacy of the fire will be lost, and a simultaneous fire, upon which a great deal depends, will not be obtained; for experience and reasoning demonstrate the fact, every thing else being equal, that platoon-firing is more effective in proportion as it is executed together. When the officer leaves a suitable interval between the commands "Aim" and "Fire," the men have time to adjust the piece to the shoulder, to place the finger in front of the trigger, and to exercise a slight pressure on the trigger when awaiting the command "Fire." They are then ready to fire the moment the command is given, thus obtaining a simultaneous and effective fire. But, if the officer superintending the firing should be careful to leave a sufficient interval between the commands "Aim" and "Fire," he should no less avoid the opposite extreme. If he keeps the men aiming too long, they will become fatigued, will lose their aim, and will not be prepared to obey the command when given. It is only by commanding, and seeing platoon and company firing executed with ball and cartridge, and judging of its effect by the number of balls put in the target, that officers can appreciate the influence of a command properly given, and acquire the habit of thus giving their commands.

When firing by file, by company or rank, or by platoon, the officers will indicate the distance which separates the company from the object to be fired at. Men in ranks are necessarily more or less constrained in their movements. Occupied, moreover, in loading their pieces, soldiers will not be able to judge the distance which separates them from the enemy.

The most suitable moment to indicate the distance will be immediately before the command "Aim" is given. The men will then be in a position to regulate the hausse. To direct the fire of a platoon upon an enemy, for example, at 400 yards, the officer will command, "Fire by platoon," "Platoon—Ready—at 400 yards—Aim—Fire—Load."

The above observations are applicable to firing by company or rank.

When firing by file, the distance will be announced immediately before the command "Commence firing," and after the command "Ready."

Inaccuracy of fire may arise from very different causes.

1st. From ignorance of, or failing to apply, the principles which govern good marksmen when firing.

2d. A ball, when fired, may be, and generally is, deflected from its course when describing the trajectory.

The first causes may be obviated in a great degree by practical and theoretical instruction.

The second is attributable to the piece, and exterior influences acting upon the ball. Some of the causes cannot be modified by the most skilful marksman; while others, to a great extent, may be counteracted. It would be unreasonable to expect comparative perfection *in every gun* issued from our large manufactories. Our rifle musket is believed to be as perfect an arm of its kind as has ever been made. A perfect arm can only exist in theory. A soldier always firing the same piece will become acquainted with its defects, and will be able to make such allowances when firing as experience teaches him to be necessary.

Among the exterior influences which affect the accuracy of a gun, the principal one is the wind. If the wind blows from the right, the ball will be deflected to the left; to the right, if it blows from the left; raised, if from the rear; and lowered, if from the front; raised and to the left, if it blows from the rear and right. The deviation produced by the wind will be increased in proportion as the distance increases: it increases even more rapidly than the distance. Experience alone can teach the soldier the allowance he must make for the wind. Not only does the wind affect accuracy of fire by deflecting the ball from its course, but it prevents a person from holding his piece steady.

The temperature and dampness of the atmosphere influence the ball in its flight. It has been remarked that in dry weather longer ranges have been obtained than in damp weather.

When firing at an object in motion, allowance must be

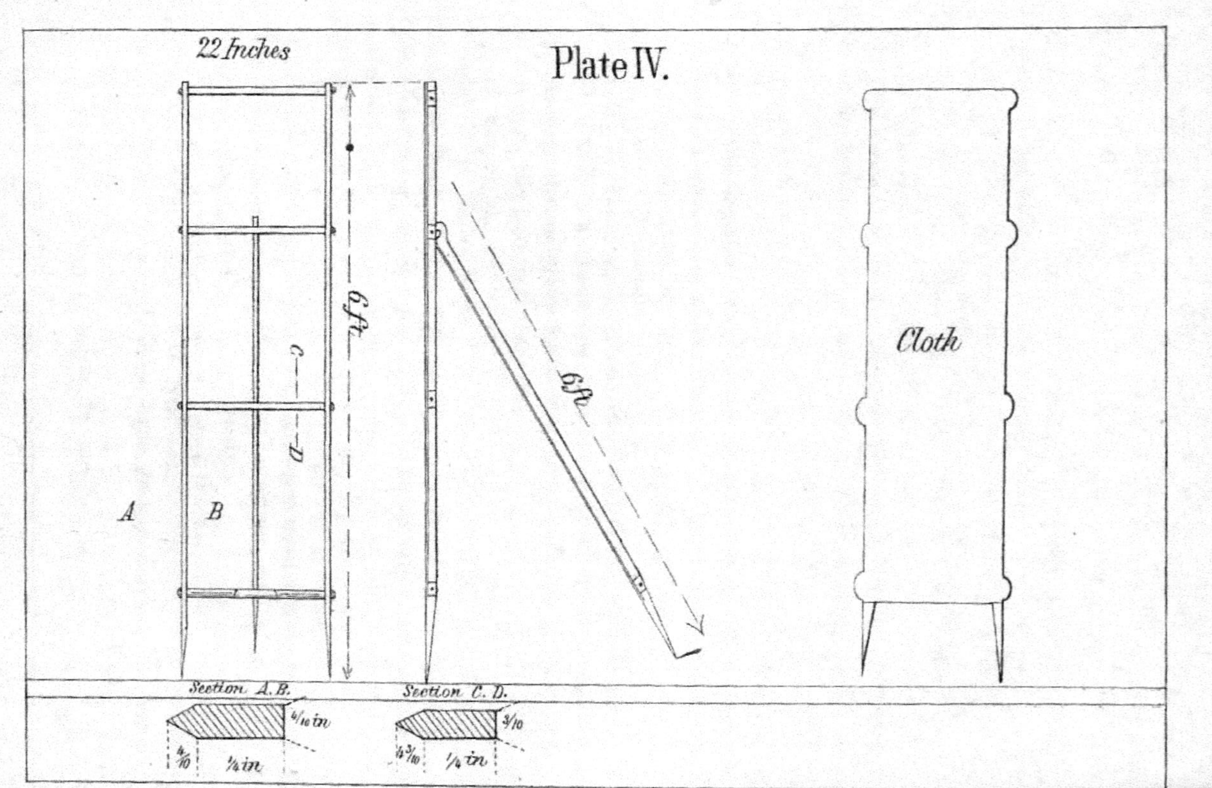

22 Inches
Plate IV.
Cloth
6 ft.
6 ft.
A
B
C
D
Section A.B.
Section C.D.
4/10 in
4/10
1/4 in
4 3/10
1/4 in
3/10

made for the motion.　For instance, when firing at a horse-man galloping in a direction perpendicular to the plane of fire, it is necessary that the line of sight should move in pro-portion as the horseman moves, and should be directed in advance of him in proportion as he is farther off.

In opening a fire upon an enemy, particular attention should be paid to discover where the first balls fired strike.　It would be better that the balls fall short of, rather than pass over, the enemy.　In the first case, we stand a chance of a ricochet ball taking effect.　From which we naturally deduce that a soldier should be impressed with the necessity of firing too low rather than too high.

Targets.

THE difficulty of procuring any specified material for targets at many posts precludes the adoption of any particular target.

The surface fired at, at the different distances, will alone be fixed by regulation.

The following suggestions are offered.

The best targets, and those recommended for permanent posts, are of cast iron,—by far the cheapest and most durable. The different surfaces required could be obtained by having four cast-iron targets of the following dimensions,—one target 6 feet by 22 inches; one 6 feet by 44 inches; one 6 feet by 66 inches; and one 6 feet by 132 inches.

When cast-iron targets cannot be had, the next best are targets formed of wrought-iron frames (see Plate 4) with muslin stretched upon them.　Four frames of the following dimensions, by combination, would enable us to obtain the sur-faces required,—one 6 feet by 22 inches; one 6 feet by 44 inches; one 6 feet by 88 inches; one 6 feet by 110 inches; and all the parts could be carried in a wagon-body.

By carefully covering the ball-holes with patches of paper pasted on, we strengthen and thicken the target; and one of these targets will last longer than one would suppose.

The next best targets are wooden frames composed of four pieces, 6 inches wide and 1 inch thick, bolted together; the ends of the vertical sides projecting about a foot below, and sharpened, the frame covered with muslin and held in position by four guys fastened to the top and attached to pins in the ground in front and rear. (See Plate 5.)

Every target, except the one used in determining the regimental prizeman, will be marked by a vertical and a horizontal stripe, dividing it into four equal parts, and varying in width according to the distance, as follows:

At	150		and	225	yards	4	inches	wide
"	250		"	300	"	5	"	"
"	325		"	350	"	8	"	"
"	400	450	"	500	"	12	"	"
"	550	600	"	700	"	16	"	"
"	800	900	"	1000	"	20	"	"

Targets will be furnished by the quartermaster's department.

Prizes.

PRIZES will be of three kinds,—an army prize, regimental prizes, and company prizes.

The company prize will be awarded by the captain, after the annual target-practice has terminated, to that non-commissioned officer, musician, or private, who has hit the target the greatest number of times at the various distances prescribed.

The company prize will be a brass *stadia*, worn on the right or left breast, according to the arm used, musket or rifle; the ball passed through the button-hole, and the hook fastened to

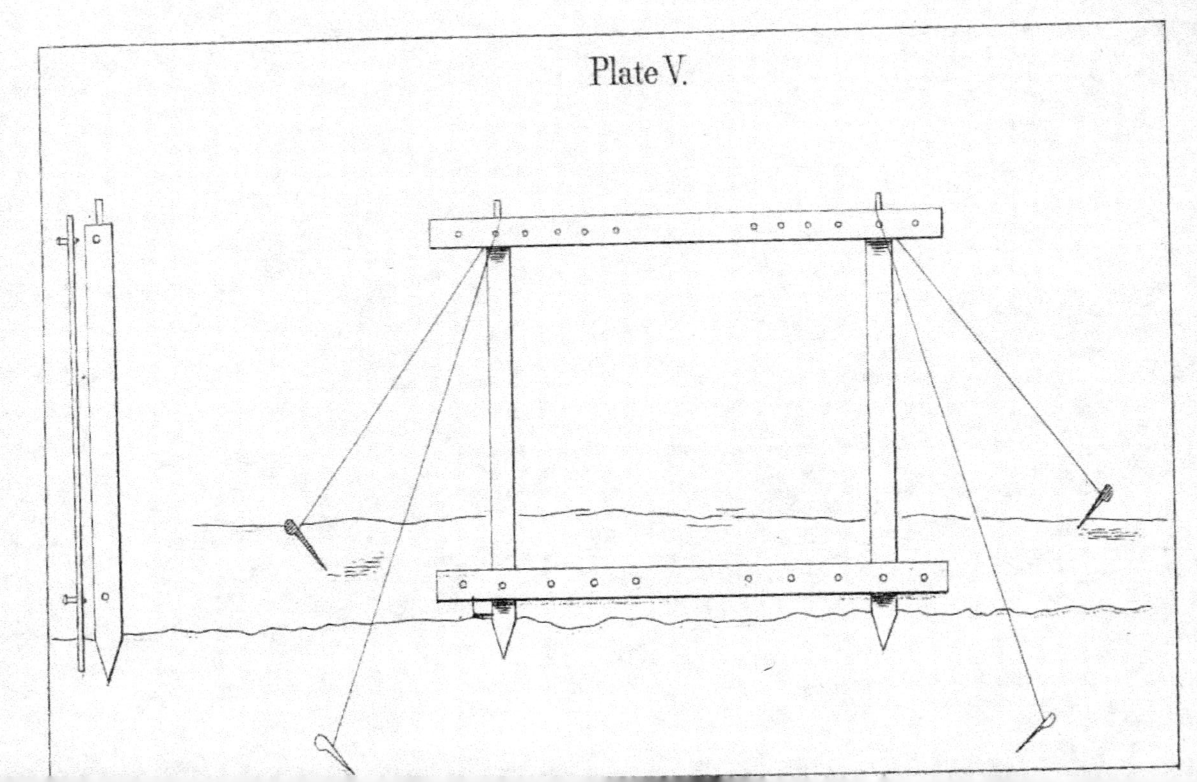

Plate V.

Plate VI.

a loop worked four inches from the row of buttons. (See Plate 6.)

Should several men of the company have the same number of hits, they will, under the supervision of the captain, fire at a target 200 yards distant until the question is decided. Should a man, from unavoidable causes, fail to fire from one or more of the prescribed distances, and if by firing from these distances he might prove the successful competitor, he will be permitted to fire under the supervision of the captain.

The regimental prize will be a silver stadia, with a silver chain attached. It will be awarded by the colonel of the regiment to that company prizeman who has made the shortest string; and his name and company will be announced in regimental orders. To enable colonels to determine the regimental prizemen, commanding officers of posts will be governed by the following regulations. The company prizemen, at each post, to fire according to the details given below, under the direction of the commanding officer, who will forward a record of the firing of the best shot of the several companies of the same regiment to regimental headquarters.

1st. The order in which the men fire will be determined by lot.

2d. The target will be a circular board or boards three feet in diameter. The middle of the target will be marked by the centre of a black circle eight inches in diameter. The rest of the target will be painted white.

3d. Each man fires ten balls. The distance fired from will be 200 yards.

4th. After each shot, the distance from the centre of the ball-hole to the centre of the target will be measured and recorded. The ball-hole is then covered by pasting over it a small piece of paper.

5th. Balls which strike by ricochet will be counted as having missed the target.

6th. Each miss counts 20 inches on a man's string. In all cases the man whose string is shortest is selected. *

7th. If several competitors obtain equal strings, they will fire as many shots as may be necessary to decide the question between them.

8th. The position fired from will be that of a soldier "firing as a skirmisher standing."

9th. Each man shall load and fire his own gun. The full charge of powder in a cartridge will be used. No allowance will be made for guns hanging fire.

The firing, if possible, should be finished in one practice or trial. However, should the weather change during the trial, and be such that it operates to the disadvantage of those whose turn it is to fire last, the commanding officer will suspend the trial, to be resumed when the weather permits.

The circular target should be raised at least three feet from the ground.

The regimental prize will be given to the successful competitor by the inspector-general, should he be present; in his absence, by the senior officer present on parade.

If two men of a regiment have the same string, the colonel will inform the commanding officer of the post or posts at which these men are stationed, who will direct an additional ten shots to be fired, and forward the record of firing as before.

Prizes will be worn on all full-dress occasions, on orderly duty, and when attending the pay-table.

Regimental and company prizes shall be held by the successful competitor until the next annual distribution takes place. A man having worn a prize for one year may obtain the prize a second, or any number of years, provided he is the successful competitor.

As prizes are honorable badges, a soldier may be deprived of them by the sentence of a general court-martial.

Prizes will be furnished by the Ordnance Department.

Plate VIII.

PRIVATE
Company
Regiment
U.S. ARTILLERY.
ARMY TARGET
Prize
18

Requisitions will be made for them by regimental commanders and company officers. They will be borne on the Ordnance-Return as other property. Soldiers will be charged with their loss, or injury, as with other public property.

The army prize will be a silver medal $2\frac{1}{2}$ inches in diameter, suspended by a silver chain.

The chain will be worn around the neck, the medal resting on the breast.

The army-prize will be worn on all full-dress occasions, on orderly duty, and when attending the pay-table.

The army prize, when awarded, belongs to the soldier, who may, however, be deprived of wearing it, by the sentence of a general court-martial.

On one side of the medal will be engraved the grade, name, company, and regiment of the soldier; on the other side will be engraved, Army Target Prize for 18—. (See Plate 8.)

The army prizeman will wear both his army and regimental prizes.

The name, company, and regiment of this man to be published in orders from the headquarters of the army, and a copy forwarded, with the army prize, to his commanding officer, to be given to him by the inspector-general, if present; otherwise, by his commanding officer on parade. This man is to be determined as follows:

Regimental commanders will forward to the headquarters of the army the name, company, and record of the firing of the regimental prizeman. Should two regimental prizemen have equal strings, the same course will be pursued as determining the regimental prizeman under similar circumstances, except that the new record of firing will be forwarded direct to the headquarters of the army by the commanding officer of the post.

N. B.—The regimental prizeman will wear the regimental prize, and turn in to his captain the company prize.

Stadia.

(See Plate 7.)

THE stadia is an instrument used for estimating distances. It is a piece of copper, or other material, with an isosceles triangle cut out of it. The upper and lower sides are graduated, and a slide works from left to right. The base of the opening is perpendicular to the sides of the instrument, and represents the apparent height of a man at a given distance, when the instrument is held horizontally at a certain distance from the eye.

In the opening A B C, A B, the base, when held vertically and at a distance—say 26 inches—from the eye, represents the apparent height of a foot-soldier with his cap on, at say 150 yards.

In order that the instrument shall always be used at the same distance from the eye, a string or chain is attached to the slide. The graduation of the sides of the instrument is made by observation or by calculation, assuming the average height of an infantry-soldier to be a certain number of inches.

To use the instrument, hold the knot at the end of the string, or the ball of the chain, between the teeth, stretch the string or chain by extending the arm, keeping the base A B of the opening vertical: pass the instrument from right to left across the field of sight, until the top of the cap and feet of the man appear to graze the sides C A and C B respectively. Move the slide to the point of apparent coincidence, and take the reading above, or below, as the case may be. This will give the distance.

The upper side of the instrument is graduated to determine the distance of foot-soldiers; the other, the distance of cavalry. In the latter case, we must regard the top of the trooper's cap and his horse's feet.

Plate VII.

Fig 2
Inf. 69 in.
1000
900
800 700 600 500
650 550 450 400
350 350
250
200
150
c
a
A
c
C
B
d
d
800 700 600 500
900 650 450 450 400 350 300
250
200
150
1000
26
K
a

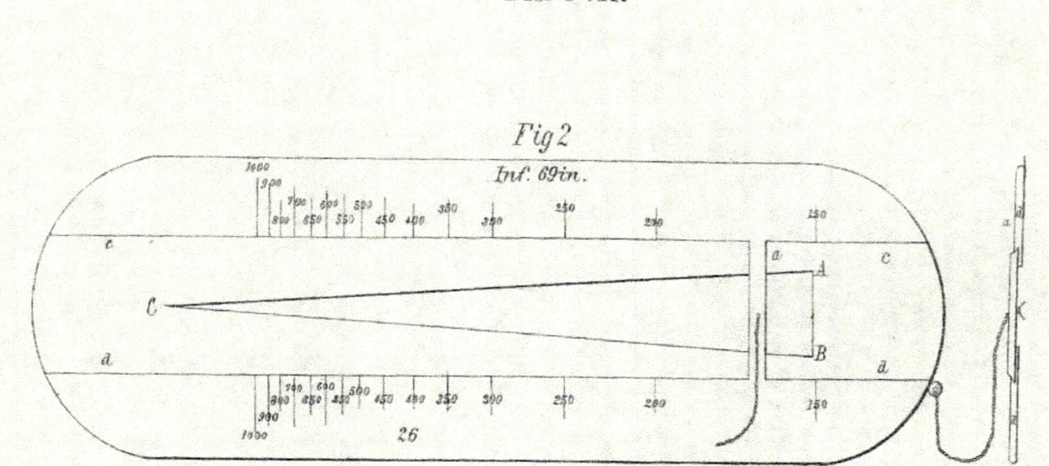

Record-Books.

EACH company will be furnished with a blankbook, two quires folio cap, in which the record of firing will be kept according to Forms I., II., and III. These books will be left at the post-adjutant's office for the inspection of the commanding officers after each firing, or at the end of the week, as that officer may direct.

Record-books will be furnished by the Quartermaster's Department, on requisitions made by commanders of companies.

The Firing of Guards.

IMMEDIATELY after the guard marches off, it will fire at a target under the supervision of the officer of the guard, or, in his absence, the officer of the day, conforming to the principles laid down in this system.

For three months in the year, commencing on the 1st of January, guards will fire at the distances 150 and 225 yards.

For three months at   "   "   250 " 300 "

"   "   "   "   "   "   325 " 350 "

"   "   "   "   "   "   400 " 450 "

When the ranges laid down above cannot be obtained, they will be approximated to as nearly as possible.

The size of the targets fired at from the several distances given above will be the same as prescribed for the same distances in Lesson II.

When practicable, the best shot will be credited with a tour of police or fatigue duty.

In this firing, the string will be measured from the centre of the ball-hole to the centre of the intersection of the horizontal and vertical stripes. Equal strings will be decided by the men firing a second shot.

FORM I.

Record of the Firing of Company "A," 1st Regiment of Infantry, 1858.

No.	FIRST-CLASS NAMES.	Grade.	150 yards.		225 yards.		250 yards.		300 yards.		325 yards.		350 yards.		400 yards.		Total No. of Hits.	No. of balls fired.	Ratio of hits to 100.
			Date.	Hits.	Date.	Hits.	Date.	Hits.	Date.	Hits.	Date.	Hits.	Date.	Hits.	Date.	Hits.			
1	A— B—	1st Sergt.	Apl. 12th	4	Apl. 19th	3	Apl. 23d	4	Apl. 26th	3	May 3d	2	May 5th	4	May 6th	4	24	28	85.71
2	C— D—	4th Sergt.	"	3	"	2	"	2	"	2	"	3	"	2	"	2	16	"	57.14
3	E— F—	Priv.	"	4	"	3	"	2	"	3	"	2	"	2	"	3	19	"	67.85
4	G— H—	"	"	*	"	3	"	3	"	2	"	3	"	2	"	2	15	24	62.05
5	I— J—	"	13th	4	"	3	"	3	"	2	4th	3	"	1	"	2	18	28	64.28
6	K— L—	"	"	4	"	3	"	2	"	3	"	2	"	2	7th	3	19	"	67.85
7	M— N—	"	"	3	"	3	"	2	"	3	"	3	"	2	"	2	18	"	64.28
8	O— P—	"	" 15th	3	"	2	" 24th	3	"	3	"	1	"	3	"	1	16	"	57.14
24	X— Y—	"	"	3	"	*	"	1	"	2	"	3	"	*	"	1	10	20	50

* Absent, sick.

FORM I, (continued.)

Record of the Firing of Company "A," 1st Regiment of Infantry, 1858.

No.	SECOND-CLASS NAMES.	Grade.	150 yards.		225 yards.		250 yards.		300 yards.		325 yards.		350 yards.		400 yards.		Total No. of Hits.	No. of balls fired.	Ratio of hits to 100.
			Date.	Hits.	Date.	Hits.	Date.	Hits.	Date.	Hits.	Date.	Hits.	Date.	Hits.	Date.	Hits.			
1	A— D—	2d Sergt.	May 8th	4	May 10th	4	May 12th	4	May 13th	4	May 15th	2	May 16th	3	May 18th	4	25	28	89.28
2	C— B—	1st Corp.	"	3	"	2	"	1	"	4	"	2	"	2	"	1	15	"	53.57
3	E— G—	3d Corp.	"	2	"	3	"	4	"	3	"	3	"	3	"	2	20	"	71.43
4	G— F—	Priv.	"	*	"	4	"	4	"	2	"	3	"	4	"	3	20	28	83.33
5	M— Y—	"	"	3	"	4	"	2	"	2	"	2	"	1	"	2	16	24	57.14
6	Q— R—	"	"	2	"	3	"	3	"	2	"	2	"	1	"	2	15	"	53.57
7	S— T—	"	"	4	11th	3	"	3	"	2	"	3	"	2	"	2	19	"	67 85
8	U— V—	"	"	3	"	4	"	3	"	4	"	3	"	3	"	3	23	"	82.14
24	W— X—	"	"	4	"	2	"	*	14th	2	"	3	"	1	"	2	14	24	58.33

* Absent, sick.

FORM I., (continued.)

Record of the Firing of Company "A," 1st Regiment of Infantry, 1858.

No.	THIRD-CLASS NAMES.	Grade.	150 yards.		225 yards.		250 yards.		300 yards.		325 yards.		350 yards.		400 yards.		Total No. of Hits.	No. of balls fired.	Ratio of hits to 100.
			Date.	Hits.	Date.	Hits.	Date.	Hits.	Date.	Hits.	Date.	Hits.	Date.	Hits.	Date.	Hits.			
1	A— C—	3d Sergt.	May 19th	4	May 20th	4	May 21st	4	May 24th	4	May 26th	3	May 27th	2	May 29th	3	24	28	85.71
2	C— B—	2d Corp.	"	4	"	4	"	2	"	3	"	4	"	3	"	2	22	"	78.57
3	T— G—	4th Corp.	"	4	"	3	22d	4	"	2	"	3	"	4	"	2	22	"	78.57
4	N— M—	Priv.	"	3	"	2	"	4	"	4	"	3	28th	2	"	4	22	"	78.57
5	H— J—	"	"	3	"	3	"	2	"	3	"	2	"	1	31st	3	17	"	60.71
6	L— O—	"	"	4	"	3	"	2	"	2	"	2	"	2	"	2	17	"	60.71
7	R— B—	"	"	3	21st	4	"	2	"	2	"	2	"	2	"	2	17	"	60 71
8	S— A—	"	"	4	"	3	"	2	"	2	"	3	"	2	"	2	18	"	64.28
24	W— C—	"	"	4	"	4	"	3	"	2	"	2	"	3	"	4	22	28	78.57

FORM I., (concluded.)

Record of the Firing of Company "A," 1st Regiment of Infantry, 1858.

No.	FIRST-CLASS NAMES.	Grade.	450 yards.		500 yards.		550 yards.		600 yards.		700 yards.		800 yards.		900 yards.		1000 yards.		Total No. of Hits.	No. of balls fired.	Ratio of hits to 100.
			Date.	Hits.	Date.	Hits.	Date.	Hits.	Date.	Hits.	Date.	Hits.	Date.	Hits.	Date.	Hits.	Date.	Hits.			
1	A— B—	1st Sergt.	Jun. 1st	3	Jun. 2d	3	Jun. 4th	2	Jun. 8th	3	Jun. 11th	2	Jun. 14th	1	Jun. 16th	0	Jun. 17th	1	15	32	46.87
2	C— D—	4th Sergt.	"	2	"	2	"	1	"	1	"	0	"	1	"	0	"	0	7	"	21.87
3	G— F—	Priv.	"	4	"	3	"	2	"	2	"	1	"	1	"	0	"	1	14	"	43.75
4	U— V—	"	"	3	"	2	"	2	"	2	"	*	"	1	"	1	"	2	13	28	46.43
5	N— M—	"	"	3	"	3	"	3	"	1	"	1	"	0	"	1	"	0	12	32	37.5
6	W— C—	"	"	3	"	2	5th	*	"	2	"	1	"	1	"	0	"	0	9	28	32.14
7	E— F—	"	"	2	"	2	"	1	"	1	"	1	"	0	"	1	"	0	8	32	25.
8	H— L—	"	"	3	3d	2	"	1	"	1	"	1	"	1	"	1	"	0	10	"	31.25
					4th		6th				12th				17th		18th				
24	S— T—	"		2	"	2	"	2	"	1	"	2	"	1	"	1	"	0	11	"	34.38

* Absent, sick.

FORM II.
Firing as Skirmishers.

1st Drill, July 1, 1858. Distance from which line of skirmishers commenced firing: 350 yards.				2d Drill, July 3, 1858. Distance from which line of skirmishers commenced firing: 600 yards.				3d Drill, July 6, 1858. Distance from which line of skirmishers commenced firing: 800 yards.			
No. of men.	No. of Balls fired.	No. of Balls hit.	Ratio per 100.	No. of men.	No. of Balls fired.	No. of Balls hit.	Ratio per 100.	No. of men.	No. of Balls fired.	No. of Balls hit.	Ratio per 100.
84	840	210	25	84	840	168	20	84	840	105	12.5

FORM III.
Firing by File, by Company or Rank, and by Platoon.

Species of Firing.	Date.	Distance.	No. of men.	No. of Balls fired.	No. of Balls hit.	Ratio per 100.
By File...............	July 15	300 yds.	84	504	290	57.54
By Rank or Company	"	"	"	168	90	53.57
By Platoon	"	"	"	168	100	59.52
Total...............				840	480	57.14
By File...............	July 17	400 yds.	81	486	215	44.24
By Rank or Company	"	"	"	162	61	37.65
By Platoon	"	"	"	162	54	33.33
Total...............				810	330	40.74
By File...............	July 18	500 yds.	79	474	161	33.97
By Rank or Company	"	"	"	158	47	29.75
By Platoon	"	"	"	158	36	22.78
Total...............				790	244	30.89

www.ingramcontent.com/pod-product-compliance
Lightning Source LLC
Chambersburg PA
CBHW052337150726

47998CB00018B/2336